Invite The Storm

C.A. Howard

Invite The Storm

Olympia Publishers
London

www.olympiapublishers.com
OLYMPIA PAPERBACK EDITION

A CIP catalogue record for this title is
available from the British Library.

ISBN: 978-1-80074-646-6

First Published in 2022

Olympia Publishers
Tallis House
2 Tallis Street
London
EC4Y 0AB

Printed in Great Britain

no matter how far.

no matter how far i may be

from your touch,

from your voice,

from your presence,

from your soul.

my heart will always

skip a beat at the sound of your name,

and pull me to you when you cross my

mind.

i hope this is love,

because, if it's not,

i am terrified of what falling for you

will actually feel like.

the way my soul

aches for you

makes me hate

loving you so

completely.

i think i am over you...

then you leave,

and my soul feels

lost without yours.

some people call me crazy

for wanting you to be happy

above all else.

even if that happiness is

not with me.

but isn't that

a part of loving someone?

giving them a piece of yourself

you may never get back?

i think i have given you

my happiness.

why am i still looking

for myself?

maybe looking is why

i can't seem to find myself.

maybe i need to live

and let myself come to me.

broken

gasping

on the floor

sobbing.

you

are

not

whole

and you don't know if

you will ever be enough.

get up.

it hurts like hell

it's harder than anything

but you are worth fighting

for

so pick up your sword

and run into the fray.

what are you running from?

yourself?

your family?

someone you know?

why are you running?

are you scared?

are you angry?

are you incapable?

what if staying

meant becoming who you are?

could you fight yourself

to better yourself?

that moment when your eyes close

when you are so exhausted

you immediately start to slumber

but shake yourself awake.

that feeling you get

like your soul has left you,

like you are dropping from the

sky.

only to suddenly crash into reality.

that is what it felt like

when i fell in love with you.

it is never looks that attract me.

looks fade.

they will never make a person.

no matter how beautiful the case

what's inside it can always be shitty.

but beautiful contents will always

make the cover seem like the most

beautiful thing you'll ever see.

i didn't find you beautiful at first.

not even a bit.

but your soul called to mine

in a way i had never

experienced before.

i saw it coming

and i chose to let it.

i chose you.

never forget that

a lost love is like

having your soul taken.

you walk around feeling empty,

searching for a new purpose.

don't worry.

you'll always find one.

how do you

tell some one

you aren't who

you once were

when they refuse

to see it in

your actions?

am i really worth it?

i will never cease to ask myself.

i hope people never cease to answer.

i am who i am

because

i was who i was.

i do what i do

because

i've done what i've done.

i go through what i

go through

because

i've gone through

what i've gone through.

sometimes i think i've

lost who i am.

but that can't be true

if i still have you.

right?

sometimes

those you love most

will leave you soul

the most torn.

it's okay to cut them off

so that you can

finally thrive.

he called me a hero.

i'd never thought

i could be one

until then.

now i don't want

to be

anything else.

as she cried in my arms,

she asked,

" what if i am not ready?

what if i fail?"

i ask, "do you trust me?

because i would never

stand you up

just to watch you

fall."

you feel that pull in your soul.

it's like there is an

animal in your chest trying

to claw its way out

and nothing you do can release it

as it continues to ravage you

from the inside out.

you feel desperate for anything

to get it out

to make it go away.

but only you can do that

and it will be there

until you can learn how.

that is agony.

that is depression.

i am organized.

i am chaos.

i am happy.

i am sad.

i am calm.

i am wild.

i am sane.

i am crazy.

i am to the world,

whatever they want to see.

i am truly,

only who

i

believe myself to be.

expectation is like an anchor

hanging from your neck

waiting for you to either

hold it up

or drown.

personally, i found freedom in

taking it off.

it's a weird thing

being embraced for

all you are.

it is like a rebirth of

sorts.one that makes

you want to leave behind

everyone you knew before

and risk it all on this new

thing you have found.

if only i was a gambler.

emotions are like a river.

sometimes they run hard

and cannot be controlled.

other times they run steady

and calm.

they can also dry up.

it's the last one that scares

me the most.

because i never know when

they will flow again

and i don't think

i am worth knowing without them.

i only own who i am

because with the shit

i've done,

would it be fair

to deny it?

i find regret to either

be a tether

or a tow.

it can either hold you

in the past.

or motivate you for

the future.

you decide.

i would ask why it is so hard

to walk away from him.

why i can't seem to let go

of this wave that crashes

over my heart at the thought

of you.

if i could, i would run.

if i could, i would leave.

i used to say i don't know

the word can't.

you taught it to me.

i wish i

could tell you

how much

i love

not

loving you

anymore.

to describe his touch

would be like describing

something that has yet

to happen.

impossible.

there are some storms that

are going to be lighter than

others.

some may be a mist.

some may be a major

hurricane.

i've found those who have

weathered a storm

to be the best kind of people.

they know not to judge, but

to accept.

mind racing.

heart pumping.

a beast in your chest trying

to get out.

you say things you

don't mean.

you do things you wouldn't,

that you know you shouldn't.

all from your stress and

anxiety.

step back.

breathe.

learn.

do you really

understand?

do you really

try?

or is that

what you tell

yourself?

because i don't

feel understood.

why some

people feel

more important

than others

is something

i will

never understand.

are we

not all

worth something?

i will help

anyone until they

prove to no

longer want it.

then you must

take a step back

and let them fail.

for some people

must learn the hard

way that they are

just human.

if he loved us

the way he said,

why was it so

easy for him to

let us leave

and hard for

him to chase

after us?

aren't parents supposed

to fight for their children?

were we not enough?

was it me?

what you see

may not be

all they are.

dig deep

and you may

find a story

worth reading.

some people wander

their whole life

trying to find

who they are.

what they need

to realize is

that they are

the prey.

not the predator.

just let it find you.

some people will never

see you for who

you are

and the value you

can bring to

their life.

brush it off.

because the people

who can see you

with 20/20

are out there.

you just have to look.

the most beautiful thing

you will ever be to me

is yourself.

how long can

a body take

emotional punches

before it

breaks down?

i'm bloody

and bruised

and i

don't know

if i can

take much more.

could i take

that step?

could i let

you love me?

i don't know

if i know

how.

when the sun

sets and all

that is left

are your thoughts

where do yours

travel?

is it somewhere

i can follow?

do people

actually live?

or do

we just

walk around

pretending.

acting.

putting on a

show.

if i promise

you my world,

are you willing

to give me

yours?

because that's

the only way

my heart

knows how to

function.

just

call my name

and i will

not listen.

call to my

soul and i

will find you

anywhere.

i don't know

if i will

fall or fly.

but at least

i can say

i took the

leap.

i wish

i could see

your thoughts.

for i wonder

if i consume

yours as well.

i may not

know where

life will take

me after this.

but i know

i am finally

happy

where i am.

i wish i knew

that while i was busy

hating the world.

i was really hating

myself.

if only

i had known then

that one day

i would be experiencing

my now.

that happiness exists

for me.